D0536037

NO LONGER
PROPERTY OF PPLD

HARLOW
&
INDIANA
(and Reese)

Also by Brittni Vega
HARLOW & SAGE (AND INDIANA)

HARLOW
&
INDIANA
(and Reese)

A True Story About Best Friends...
and Siblings Too!

———

BRITTNI and JEFF
VEGA

G. P. PUTNAM'S SONS
New York

PUTNAM

G. P. PUTNAM'S SONS
Publishers Since 1838
An imprint of Penguin Random House LLC
375 Hudson Street
New York, New York 10014

Copyright © 2015 by Brittni and Jeff Vega
Penguin supports copyright. Copyright fuels creativity, encourages diverse voices, promotes free speech, and creates a vibrant culture. Thank you for buying an authorized edition of this book and for complying with copyright laws by not reproducing, scanning, or distributing any part of it in any form without permission. You are supporting writers and allowing Penguin to continue to publish books for every reader.

ISBN 978-1-101-98367-6

Printed in the United States of America

1 3 5 7 9 10 8 6 4 2

Book design by Jan Derevjanik

FOR OUR
BEST FRIEND,
SAGE

This is a true story. Well, most of it.

My name is Indiana. I am a Miniature Dachshund, although I don't feel very miniature. People always think that I am so petite, but take a good look at me. I am certainly not "miniature." I have felt larger than life since the day I was born.

Come on in! I want to tell you my story.

I was born on a hot summer night, in an old red barn out in the middle of nowhere. My birth parents were both rodeo dogs and traveled everywhere with their beloved pet horses. They weren't around much, so I spent the first few weeks of my life in the barn with my littermates, a small group of chickens, and a retired show horse named Old Thunderbolt. I didn't fit in with anyone in the barn except Old Thunderbolt (she was just my size!), so I followed her everywhere.

"You can't stay with me forever, little one," Thunderbolt told me one day over hay.

"Why not?" I asked.

"Because you have a family somewhere out there that is waiting to meet you. You'll see," she said.

Sure enough, she was right. There was a family out there that was waiting for me.

When I was exactly eight weeks old, a nice couple came to the barn to visit. I took one look at them and knew that they were mine. Then I showed them that they were mine by sitting on their laps and not moving. They must have felt the same way about me because the next thing I knew, they were signing my adoption papers and loading me into their station wagon.

"You be good, little one," Old Thunderbolt yelled to me as we rode off into the sunset.

My new mother looked down at me and asked, "Are you ready to go home?"

"You bet!" I said. But I don't think she heard me . . . Humans are funny that way.

I spent the long car ride home gazing out the window and eating treats. I loved these people and their car with their air-conditioning and all of their treats. What a life!

It took us a few hours, but eventually we arrived at my new home. My castle. My fortress. All mine.

And that is when I met Harlow.

That's Harlow. Isn't she a gem?

Like Old Thunderbolt, Harlow was just my size.
I knew from the moment I saw her that we were
going to be best friends.

But she had other things in mind.

At first, I don't think she liked me.

After I unpacked my suitcase and got settled in, my parents sat down and stared at me, trying to come up with a name. The name on my birth certificate read: Princess Buttercup. I hated it. I wanted a name that people would take a little bit more serious, such as Elizabeth, Harriet, Joan, or Madonna.

"No offense, but you don't really look like a Princess Buttercup," my father said.

"She doesn't look like a princess at all," Harlow mumbled as she glared at me from the corner.

"She's such an adventurous little thing," my mother said as I climbed all over the furniture, exploring my new territory. "Let's call her Indiana Sage. Indi for short."

The name Sage was a tribute to an older sister that I never got to meet.

Up until a few weeks before my arrival, Sage had been Harlow's best friend. But, like all dogs do, Sage moved on to a better place when her body was old and stopped working.

Sage was one of a kind.

"Next to Lassie, she was the greatest dog who had ever lived," Harlow would tell me later on.

Even though dogs don't wear shoes, I knew right away that Sage had left some pretty big shoes to fill, and I was just the dog to do it!

It took Harlow a few weeks to warm up to me. But eventually she came around. And we have been inseparable ever since.

I know, I know. I was so small back then! I grew up to be much bigger than Harlow in size, but . . . she is still the "big sister" and I am the "little sister." And everything that I know, I have learned from her.

We established from the very beginning that I was in charge. Yes, Harlow knew much more than I did, but I am the boss. I was just born that way. Harlow didn't seem to mind and neither did my parents. I had them all wrapped around my little ~~finger~~ paw. I mean, just look at me! Have you ever seen a cuter face?

(I didn't think so.)

Part One:
Harlow &
Indiana

"Indiana! Your breath smells awful!
Did you not have your canines brushed before bed last night?"
Harlow asked the moment I opened my eyes
and had my morning yawn.

Having my teeth brushed is not something that I enjoy. It is a task that requires both parents. First, my mother lures me into the washroom with a treat, and then, from the corner, my father comes out and scoops me up before I can say, "Pig's ear!" Together they work to clean each and every tooth in my mouth while Harlow stands by and watches.

"You missed one," she says.

But as always, my parents never understand her.

"Harlow, how come we can understand them, but they can't understand us?" I had asked when I was just a small puppy.

"Because, Indiana, dogs are the most intelligent creatures on planet Earth," she replied.

For the record, on that particular morning, I had not had my teeth brushed the night before. Harlow and I had stayed up late watching our shows, and by the time we crept into our parents' room for bed, they were both already snoring.

Harlow and I have always had our own bed, but we prefer to sleep in our parents' bed. The thought of sleeping so close to the ground is disturbing. And Harlow has a bad back, for goodness' sake!

Lilly & Abbie

I had always assumed that eventually my parents would take the hint and start sleeping in our bed on the floor so that we wouldn't have to fight them for space every night. But so far, they hadn't, and each night had been a struggle. Or so it seemed for *them*, at least. Harlow liked to sleep on my father's right side and I opted for his left side, creating the perfect Daddy sandwich.

"I. Can't. Move," he would say every morning when the rooster on his phone would go off.

"You two would be much more comfortable in your own bed," my mother had tried to explain.

Such a sweet woman, I thought. Parents, they just don't understand.

Besides, after they get up and leave for the day, the big bed is all ours anyway. We spend more time there than they do. We have every right to sleep there whenever we want.

DOG LIFE

Five days a week, Harlow and I do the same thing. Sleep late, watch television, stare at the mail carrier from the window,

play with our toys (de-stuffing and de-squeaking), and do some research on the iPad (mostly cat videos), which is very hard to master when you don't have fingers!

At 5:30 p.m. sharp, we sit patiently at the top of the stairs, listening for the garage door to open and waiting for our parents to come walking through the door. We like to be the first things they see after a long day at the office!

At dinner, I do my absolute best
to look extra-cute so that I can get
additional food.

(It almost always works.)

After dinner, my father puts on his running shoes and my mother puts on our leashes and we take our evening walk.

My job is to protect my family from random passersby.

"Oh, what an adorable little dog you have!" or "That's so cute! A big one and a little one!" people say as we are walking. That is when I go into full attack mode!

"Who are you calling 'little'? That's my sister!" I yell at them.

"Indiana! Quit your barking!" my mother warns.

Harlow has always been unfazed by strangers. She seems happy to meet anyone, which is fine, as long as I am around to protect her and keep her safe.

But most of the time, it's just me and my Harlow, hanging out at home.

WHAT'S YOURS IS MINE

I learned early on that everything of Harlow's is mine as well. There are no boundaries.

Harlow is one smart ~~cookie~~ biscuit. She is very knowledgeable and knows everything about everything, which is perfect because I was born with a lot of questions.

"Can cats and dogs become best friends?"

"Of course they can. Don't you remember the movie *The Adventures of Milo and Otis*?" Harlow replied. "Just stay clear of Siamese cats, especially if they are in pairs. Trouble."

"Have you ever caught your own tail?"

"Never," Harlow said sadly. "But trust me, I have spent many years trying."

Harlow was a pro at sharing her knowledge, and I have kept a mental note of everything she has said. You never know, one day I might need it.

The best thing about being the baby sister is the collection of toys I inherited the day that I moved in. All of Harlow's toys became my toys.

At first Harlow threw a fit.

"Harlow! You share," my parents would scold her.

"Whatever!" she yelled.

"Bark at me one more time and I will donate every single toy to the Humane Society!" my mother had threatened.

And so Harlow had tried to teach me about sharing. She would play with the smaller toys and watch as I played with the bigger toys— her toys.

"You see, isn't sharing fun, Indiana?"

Why, yes, it was fun. But then I decided that I wanted the smaller toys as well as the bigger toys. I wanted all of the toys, so I took each one of them to my side of the room.

"I am sharing," I explained. "I am sharing all of your toys with myself."

"No, Indi. That is not how it works. If you are going to play with my toys, I am going to play with yours."

Harlow, as smart as she is, can be so silly sometimes.

THE HOLIDAY

Weekends at my house are spectacular occasions. We get to sleep late, have pancakes for breakfast, and, most important, go on family adventures!

Sometimes we take a quick trip over to the hardware store. Harlow hates going because all of the gentlemen there assume that (a) she is a boy, and (b) she is a hunting dog.

"I am not a hunting dog!" she yells.

"Harlow! Don't bark. That's not like you, old gal," my father always whispers to her.

If anything, I am the hunter in the family. Missing shoe? I can always find it. It is probably at the bottom of my toy box. Harlow's favorite

Nylabone goes missing? I know just where I placed it! Spider living in the garage? I will take care of that right away!

One Friday afternoon, my parents came home from work early. They loaded the family station wagon with suitcases, coolers, and some of our toys.

"I hope they aren't taking us to the pound," Harlow said to me as we both watched.

"Don't be silly, Harlow!" I replied. "I can't even remember the last time we got in trouble."

"Get in the car, ladies! We are going on a family vacation!" my father announced.

The journey started out fun. Harlow had her head out the window like she always did when we rode in the car.

"You are going to get a bug in your mouth," I tried to tell her.

She never listened. Hanging my head out the window while the car is in motion has never been my cup of tea. Instead, I enjoy the scenery from inside the car and give my parents directions from the backseat. I am the perfect backseat driver!

Our first stop was at a place called Wendover. (One of many restroom breaks.) I did my business while my father gassed up the car. My mother was solving a crossword puzzle and Harlow was listening to her Walkman. That's when I saw something from the corner of my eye . . . a fifty-foot cowboy! It was in that moment that I realized I was in for a real adventure.

THE TWILIGHT ZONE

Later that night, we watched the sun set from a
beautiful place called Lake Tahoe. Fresh air, lots of
grassy areas, and the biggest water bowl I had ever
seen! It was such a beautiful place.

It was there that we settled in for the night.

And that is when things got strange, real strange.

We pulled into the parking lot at midnight.

"Remember, girls, best behavior,"
my mother said as we got
out of the car.

I had never seen anything like it. Bates, the sign outside the old building read. *Why does that sound familiar?* I wondered.

When we walked into the building, a man wearing a tuxedo greeted us.

"Welcome, Harlow and Indiana! Let's get you to your room."

Together, we all stood in a silver box, which looked like an oversized microwave. As you can imagine, I was frightened.

"It's okay, Indi. This is an elevator," Harlow whispered.

When the microwave doors finally opened, we were on a different floor. (Yes, very *Twilight Zone*-y, I know.)

The man used a CARD (not keys) to open the door to our room.

"Here we are, room 1408. Sleep tight, don't let the bedbugs bite!" he said, winking at me as he turned around and left.

I was officially scared.

Harlow and my parents made themselves comfortable on the bed in our room.

"How can you just go to sleep?" I asked Harlow. "This is not our bed. I can smell strangers on this bed! We don't even have cable in here!"

"Oh, Indiana. Go to sleep," Harlow said sleepily as my father turned off the light.

I stood guard all night. I kept my eyes on the door to our room. Outside our room, I could hear people walking around. *Zombies,* I thought. *What kind of vacation is this?*

27

I must have fallen asleep, because at six a.m., I was awakened by the sound of growling in the hallway.

"Ahhhhhh! Make it stop. Make it stop!" I screamed.

28

"Indi! Shhh. It is just a vacuum," Harlow said, clearly annoyed.

"I want to go home!" I shouted.

"Indiana! Quit barking. You are going to wake up the neighbors!" my mother whispered.

"Someone is vacuuming at six a.m.!" I screamed. "The neighbors are probably already awake!"

We got up, ate our kibble, and waited. Even Harlow was ready to leave.

THE SAN FRANCISCO TREAT

"Next stop, San Francisco!"
my father announced as I watched the old
hotel disappear in the rearview mirror.

I slept the whole way there, in the safety
of my father's arms.

San Francisco is a magnificent place. By day two, I had finally gotten used to staying in a hotel. (Although I did prefer to use my own pillow and blanket.)

We visited the ocean for the first time, and since Sage had never been to the ocean, we brought her along too. She is always with us in spirit. When I was just a small puppy, Harlow explained that Sage's collar is something she called our family's "good-luck charm."

I learned how to use a camera and got some great pictures of Harlow's . . . eyes.

Sticking my tongue out for photographs is something that I learned from Harlow. When she doesn't want her picture to be taken, out comes her tongue. She thinks it is the funniest thing on earth. My mother doesn't think it is very funny, so naturally I started doing it too, just to spice things up.

Harlow and I, we are pretty decent animals. We don't cause trouble. At least not when we are out in public. That is why it was so shocking when Harlow had a run-in with the law.

It all started out very pleasantly. We were having a nice family picnic on the beach. A seagull must have distracted me when Harlow wandered off.

"Where is Harlow?" my mother asked in a panic.

The three of us ran up and down the beach looking for her, but she was nowhere to be found.

This is what happens when you let a six-year-old off her leash! I thought, glaring at my parents.

"Oh, my word! There!" My mother pointed to a police car.

Oh, no, I thought. *It can't be. Not Harlow!* She was the golden child in the family! But it was Harlow, all right, sitting in a police car. Probably paw-cuffed. Harlow had gotten herself arrested!

"Is this your dog?" the police officer asked my parents.

"Yes," my parents both said, rightfully ashamed.

"We took her in because she was eating out of people's picnic baskets."

My parents quickly moved from shame to utter humiliation.

Luckily, Harlow got off with a warning and we got to enjoy the rest of our time in San Francisco . . . on leashes, of course.

I thought for sure that we would be heading home when we left our hotel on the beach, but my mother and father thought otherwise.

"Who wants to go to Hollywood?" my father asked.

"He means Harlowood," Harlow said with a wink.

Who are we? I thought. *The Griswolds?*

PLANET HARLOWOOD

Just like San Francisco,
Los Angeles was lovely. Except for
one small thing: traffic.

For two hours, I waited to use the restroom
while we sat at a dead stop on the highway.

"Oh, come on! Why aren't we moving?"
I complained.

Harlow gave me a brief lesson
on rush hour and traffic jams.

"Why don't people just ride horses?" I asked.

Harlow didn't respond. She just stood
there with her head out the window
like she always does.

So we sat quietly, not moving, for another hour.

But when we finally got out of the car,
it was beautiful!

Meryl Streep is kind of a big deal in our family. She practically raised Harlow and Sage, and I had learned a thing or two from watching her movies as well.

"Let's go and find Meryl's paw prints!" Harlow begged.

Somehow, my parents understood her pleas. Or it was already on the agenda. I don't know, but finding Meryl's paw prints was exactly what we set out to do!

Hollywood Boulevard is an interesting place full of very interesting people. While we were walking, a human being barked at me. I didn't know what to do, so I hid behind my mother.

"Now you know how people feel when you bark at them," Harlow whispered.

We found Meryl's paw prints. They were magnificent, just like her. (There is no photo evidence of this because I was too afraid to get down on the ground and pose for a picture.)

After a few days in Hollywood, we moved on to San Diego.

I knew that I would love San Diego because that is where my great-grandmother Gladdiss lives. She is a lovely lady. When she visits my house, she always comes prepared with a handkerchief full of dog treats in her pocket, and when I try to take them out of her pocket she says, "Oh, hold your horses, Alabama!" (She thinks my name is Alabama.)

Harlow told me that Gladdiss once had brunch with the legendary film star Clark Gable, but I have yet to confirm this. All I know is that my great-grandma is the most wonderful human who ever lived! When I get to be her age, I hope that I look just like her!

Our hotel in Southern California was right on the beach and it was perfect.

Harlow got to do a little bird-watching.

And I stood around and looked cute.

We caught some rays in a beach chair.

And some *ZZZ*'s in a lounge chair.

At the end of the day, we enjoyed the view.

And before I knew it, our time in California had
come to an end. I was sad to say good–bye.
So was Harlow.

VEGAS VACATION

On our way home from California, we stopped in a place called Las Vegas. If you haven't heard of it, let me tell you what it is like . . . Oh, wait, I WOULDN'T KNOW! I missed the whole experience because I was sound asleep in the backseat of the car.

Harlow, however, got the full effect of Las Vegas.

She stood wide-eyed with her head out the window while my father drove up and down the strip.

"It was unlike anything I had ever seen before, Indi!" she told me the next day. "Christmas lights everywhere you look and people dressed in Halloween costumes on each corner!"

I think she was genuinely shocked by Las Vegas because she had that wide-eyed look on her face for a whole week after we came home.

My father had this same look, but I think it was because he was upset. He put a dollar into a vending machine, and instead of dispensing a soft drink like vending machines usually do, it lit up and spit out two hundred gold coins. I would be upset too.

HOME SWEET HOME

Everything returned to normal once we got home. My parents had to go back to work (such a huge adjustment for me!), and it took about six months to get caught up on laundry, but other than that, everything was business as usual.

I learned a lot of interesting things on our first family vacation, but the most important was that no matter where I go, as long as I am with my best friend, I am happy. Home is where the ~~heart~~ Harlow is!

Harlow and Indiana

HARLOWEEN

Halloween—or Harloween, as we refer to it—
is the best holiday of the entire year at our house.
Instead of dusting away cobwebs, my father goes
to the store and buys them.

"It's okay, Indiana. They are just decorations,"
Harlow told me.

"But why? Why would you want cobwebs on the
table? Or in all corners of the house?"

"Because it adds to the spooky effect!"
Harlow explained.

I wasn't buying it. After my father spent hours
cobwebbing every surface of the house, I went ahead
and de-cobwebbed so that my mother wouldn't have
to. My parents weren't very appreciative of my help.
(Last favor I do for those two.)

I don't remember my first Harloween,
because I was still just a puppy.

"You dressed me up as WHAT?" I asked Harlow.

"A big-horned sheep! Well, actually, you were a little-horned sheep, but that's not the point."

Let me be very honest with you. I don't like dressing up. I don't like wearing sweaters or hats or booties. I am a dog. I was born in the wild. I am very against animals mocking other animals by wearing their outfits.

However, when Harlow showed me the costumes that she had selected for our second Halloween together, I have to admit I was intrigued.

"Dinosaurs!" she said proudly.

Wow! Now, this was something that I could wear and be proud of. Just like me, dinosaurs were fierce. I won't lie, when I look in the mirror and I see my short little arms, I am immediately reminded of the great and powerful carnivorous Tyrannosaurus rex.

"I'm really sorry, though, Indi," Harlow said. "They didn't have the Tyrannosaurus rex costume in your size. Just mine. But I did find this green dinosaur costume for you in the cat department. It looks like it will fit you perfectly."

And so for Halloween I was a Triceratops. A plant-eating sweetheart of a creature, Triceratops.

Unfortunately, the children didn't run from me when we went trick-or-treating, like I had hoped.

A DAY TO FORGET

"Who wants to go buh–bye?" my mother and father asked one day.

"Me! Me! ME!" I screamed while raising my paw!

"Okay, Indiana. Settle down. Harlow, you wait here. We will be back soon," my father said.

I felt so special. Going for a car ride all by myself! We were probably going to the pet store. Or the bank! Either way, I knew there would be treats involved. Treats and laughter!

Imagine my disappointment when we pulled up to the veterinarian's office, a place that I despise and hadn't visited since completing my puppy vaccinations a few months before. Puppy shots are no laughing matter and remain the worst memory from my childhood!

We walked into the facility and I took one sniff and immediately started shaking like a leaf.

"It's okay, honey. It's okay, angel," my father whispered.

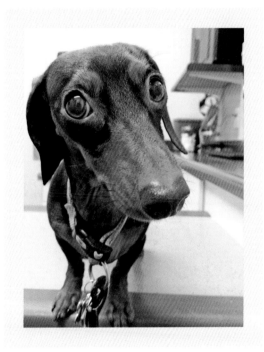

I am "Indiana" ninety-nine percent of the time, so when my father calls me my pet names, "honey" and "angel," I instantly know that all is wrong in the universe.

The nurse came in to the exam room and took my vitals. I glared at her the whole time. After she finished, she tried to make me feel better by giving me a treat from a jar.

I took it and then spit it out. (That will show her.)

"All right, Indiana. You be a good girl," my father said before handing me off to the nurse.

Hold the phone! You are just going to leave me here? Your youngest child? Your baby girl? Your honey angel?

And then the doctor came in. He had flowing brown hair and the most beautiful blue eyes. His name tag read McDREAMY.

McDreamy looked at me, and with a laugh he said, "Indiana, you are going to get very sleepy. Very sleeeeeeeeeppppppy."

And the rest was a complete blur.

When I woke up, I was in . . . a cage. *Oh, my goodness!* I thought. *What is this? Am I a bird now? Indiana does not belong in a cage!*

I spent the whole night in that cage. Scared. Alone. And very sleepy.

The next thing I remember was waking up in my parents' car.

"What a good girl, Indiana! You were so brave," my mother said to me.

Was this a dream? I felt great, like I was flying. And everything seemed so funny to me.

I turned to my mother. "Turn up the music, darlin'! I want to hear some tunes!"

When we got home, Harlow took one look at me and said, "Congratulations, Indi. You have just done your part to help control the pet population."

I didn't know what that meant. I didn't care. I curled up in my bed and slept for two days straight.

And when I woke up,
I felt better than ever.

THE DRAGON

I remember the first time I saw it. They kept it hidden in the hall closet.

On special occasions, it came out, and it was so vicious it took both hands for my mother to carry it up and down the stairs. I chased it from room to room, biting it when I had the chance. It was fast, though, much faster than me.

"Indiana, what are you going to do if you actually catch it?" Harlow asked.

She was not scared of it. Or amused.

"I am going to make sure it leaves our house and never comes back!" I said, zooming by her.

The dragon has a sidekick. A much smaller, less noisy little sidekick. I don't know what this creature is called, but during Halloween, I saw witches riding around on them like horses.

I wonder how long these two had been living in the closet before I moved in . . .

Some nights, when I couldn't sleep, I would sit outside the closet. I knew that they could see me.

The dragon and the witch's horse were my worst enemies. I hoped for the day when my parents would come to their senses and remove both of them from our home.

SCAREDY-DOGS

Harlow, bless her heart, is afraid of thunder. I find it so silly.

If it is raining, you can most likely find her hiding underneath a piece of furniture or in the shower behind the curtain.

Harlow has hiding spots all over the house. Sometimes we turn this into a game.

I am now going to tell you how our game works. Take notes so you can play at home too.

First I close my eyes and I begin to count while Harlow goes and hides. When I reach one hundred, I yell, "Ready or not, here I come!" That is when I open my eyes and start seeking. I call this game hide-and-seek.

One rainy Monday, I thought that Harlow and I were playing our game and that she had just forgotten to tell me, because from eight o'clock in the morning until five o'clock that evening, I was searching for her.

Little did I know, Harlow wasn't hiding from me, she was hiding from the thunder.

When my father got home from work, he frantically searched each room.

"Harlow! Harlow! Come on, Harles! Indiana, where is your sister?" he asked.

We could not find her anywhere. And the sound of the thunder outside was getting louder and louder.

Thoughts of being an only child began to cross my mind. As much as I loved the idea of all the attention being an only child would bring me, I couldn't bear the thought of life without Harlow! She is my best friend.

Alert the authorities, I thought. *We have to find my sister!*

We searched. And searched. And finally, the thunder stopped.

By this time, my mother was home and was helping with our search party.

I knew when Harlow had been found because both of my parents started laughing, and when I ran upstairs, I could see why.

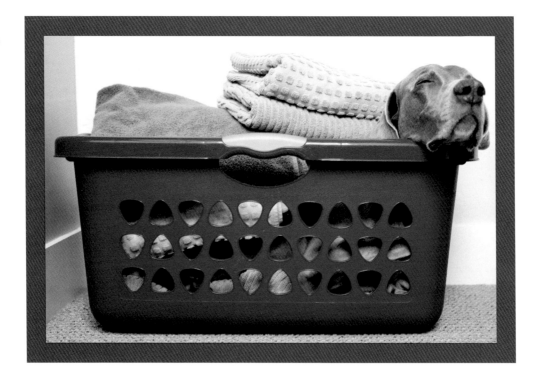

WHEN LIFE HANDS YOU LEMONS

I don't want to brag, but . . .
I have quite the collection of toys.

I have my "babies," which are stuffed and
make a squeaking noise when I carry them in
my mouth. I have my "chews," which help keep
my teeth clean and strong. Last but certainly not
least, I have my tennis balls. I love each
one of them and I keep them scattered around
the house, at least one in each room. I even keep
a few hidden in the backseat of the car.
They are my pride and joy.

Part Two:
Harlow & Indiana
(and Reese)

THE BABY

I will be the first to admit it. I loved being the baby in the family. Sure, I like to act tough, but deep down, I really like being the most special member of the family: Daddy's little angel. Momma's pride and joy. Harlow's baby sister.

There are so many perks.

I'm not proud of this, but sometimes I would even use birth order to manipulate my parents.

Garbage scattered all over the kitchen because I decided to go dumpster diving? I just sit back, put on my most innocent face, and watch as Harlow takes the blame.

New shoes chewed to tiny pieces because I was feeling a little bored?

"She did it!" I say, pointing my long nose in Harlow's direction.

Harlow loves me, even when I get her in trouble. And I love her. I don't know what we would do without each other. We are best friends, two peas in a pod, and even though I am just a little bit bossy, Harlow adores me and I love being her sidekick.

Life for the two of us was pretty much perfect.

Until it arrived.

NOBODY PUTS INDI IN THE CORNER

Harlow and I were having a cuddle on the couch when the garage door opened.

"They are home early," Harlow said as she got up and stretched.

"Hopefully they have something fun planned for us!"

My father came in first and sat down on the couch. "Hello, ladies! We have a surprise for you!"

A surprise? I thought. *I love surprises!* I was so overjoyed that I barely noticed my mother walk in. She sat down beside him. She was holding a blanket. I couldn't see what was inside it.

"Oh, my goodness, Harlow! I bet there is something really special in that blanket!" I screamed.

"I hope it's a new toy!" Harlow yelled.

"Harlow! Indiana! Both of you settle down. You don't want to frighten her," my mother told us.

Her? I thought.

"We have a new family member that is going to live with us," my father explained.

"Grandma!" I yelled. My grandmother was coming to live with us! I was so excited I could hardly contain myself! "Show your face, Grandmother!" I said as my mother opened the blanket to reveal what was hiding inside.

"That's not Grandma," I whispered in horror.

"Oh, no," Harlow sighed.

REESE LIGHTNING

The creature in the blanket was unlike anything I had ever seen before. It was polka-dotted and small, small enough to be the stuffed cow that I had been destroying all week. However, unlike my cow, it wasn't making a squeaking noise. Instead, it sat silently, staring at me and Harlow.

"Why isn't it moving?" I whispered to Harlow.

"I don't know. Smell it," she replied.

I got close enough to give it a smell. It had a strange scent. I couldn't quite put my paw on it.

"Puppy breath," Harlow said.

"It smells awful," I said.

"What do you think, girls?" my father asked. "Her name is Reese Lightning. She is a Miniature Dachshund, just like you, Indiana."

I was speechless. Harlow was too.

"Reese Lightning is your new sister," my father continued.

"I don't think they understand," my mother said and laughed.

Oh, we understood. We just weren't very happy about it.

UNWANTED GUEST

"Make it leave!" I begged.

"Indiana, no barking. Be nice. You will scare Reese!" my mother warned.

"Harlow, what is happening?" I asked. "What is going on? Why is this creature here, in our home, sitting on our furniture?"

I was so upset.

"I think she is scared of it," I heard my mother tell my father from the next room.

"Just give them time. Remember how Harlow acted when we brought Indiana home?" my father replied. "She was not very happy."

Reese Frightening was nothing like me. When my parents brought me home, I was a sweet bundle of joy. Everyone loved me. Especially Harlow. (Well, kind of.)

I needed time to think and some space to clear my mind. This was the worst day of my life. Without being told, I went to a place that I hadn't gone to since I chewed apart the remote control for the TV. I went to my time-out corner and sat in my thinking chair.

I spent the entire night in my corner. I did not eat dinner. I did not eat my late-night snack. I even passed on watching an episode of my favorite show, *House Hunters*. I had to figure out how to get rid of Reese Frightening.

The next day when I woke up, I noticed the new puppy lying down beside Harlow. I glared at Harlow. "Traitor," I said under my breath.

"No growling, Indi," said my dad.

"I hate everyone!" I screamed as I ran back to my corner. I was going to spend this day and every day for the rest of my life in my time-out chair!

Harlow followed me there. "Indiana, you are being very rude," she said.

I didn't look at her. Up until yesterday, we had been Lucy and Ethel. Simon and Garfunkel. Chandler and Joey. Now what were we supposed to be? The Three Stooges? *News flash, Harlow and family: three's a crowd!* I thought.

"Reese is scared, Indiana. This is the first time she has ever been away from her mother. Unlike you, she is very shy."

Reese had seemed a little bit shy, which I found very odd. The day that I came to live here, I had made myself quite comfortable. I had immediately unpacked all my belongings and marked my territory in a few different places. I never felt scared.

Ugh, leave it to Harlow to make me feel guilty. She always had to be the D. J. Tanner of the house.

"Now, come on downstairs and get to know her. You just might like her," Harlow suggested. "She's really sweet."

Instead of getting to know Reese when we went downstairs, I did something else. While Reese was playing with one of her new babies, I walked up and grabbed it from her.

EVICTED

Over the next few days, I came up with different ways to have Reese Frightening removed from my home.

The first involved her food dish, which just so happened to be my old food dish.

"Is she eating out of my bowl?" I screamed when I walked into the kitchen for dinner one evening. "Have you ever heard of germs, little dog?"

"Have you ever heard of manners?" Harlow asked me.

"Quit being such a saint, Harlow. You know how unsanitary that is."

Reese didn't stop eating.

If there was one thing that I knew for certain, it was that Reese liked food. And nothing stood in her way of eating. Which is why I moved Reese's food bowl to the front door. I was hoping that if I got her close enough to the front door, I would be able to just push her out. For good.

My plan didn't work.

Sometimes when my parents have company that stays too long, my mother excuses herself to go upstairs for a few minutes. One night I followed her so that I could see what she was doing. I watched as she turned the thermostat up as high as it would go. She winked at me when she saw me watching. Within minutes of her doing this, our guests began to sweat and look uncomfortable.

"It's late. We should probably get going," they said as they stood up and practically ran to the front door.

What a wonderful trick, I had thought.

But when I tried to use it on Reese, I failed. If there is one thing a Dachshund loves, it is to be uncomfortably warm. (I should have known.)

I was beyond excited when my mother invited me to tag along when it was time for Reese to get her first set of puppy shots. If

a trip to the vet didn't make Reese Frightening want to run for the hills, I didn't know what would!

This is it, I thought. *After this terrible experience, Reese will pack up her little suitcase and move out of my house!*

But as always, things didn't go as planned.

"Oh, my goodness! She is the sweetest thing I have ever seen!" the vet technician said with a gasp. Soon all of the doctors and nurses and technicians gathered around Reese like the pup-arazzi.

Reese seemed to be enjoying all the attention. She was having the time of her life at what should have been the most terrifying place on the planet.

No, no, no. No! This was not how things were supposed to go.

73

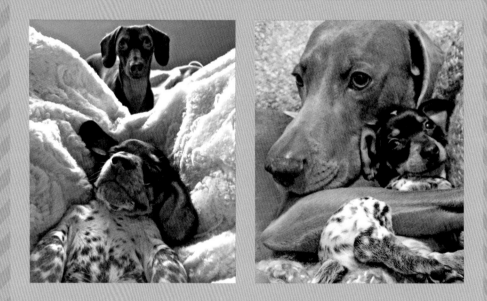

GETTING TO KNOW YOU

I couldn't quite figure Reese out. I watched everything she did from my corner. She was such an interesting little animal. She followed my parents everywhere and she loved being picked up by them. She would whine when they set her down. What a baby, right? But my parents seemed smitten by her behavior and I had obviously been forgotten about.

You know who else was completely head-over-paws in love with Reese? Harlow. Instead of finding her inconvenient and annoying, Harlow seemed to be enchanted by the little vermin. And, natch, Reese felt the same way about Harlow.

Who am I, Jan Brady? I wondered.

I wasn't used to not being the favorite. I had always been the center of attention. As much as I wanted Reese to pack her bags and leave, I was beginning to realize that she was never going to. I had to get over it or I would be an outcast in my own home.

So after ten whole days (that's almost three months for a dog!) I decided it was time to introduce myself to Reese Frightening. Formally introduce myself, that is.

Tomorrow, I decided, as I got ready for bed. Tomorrow I will introduce myself to Reese.

Reese was lying down on my parents' bed. Probably getting her beauty rest. (She needed it.)

I climbed up onto the bed, sat down beside her, and put out my paw for a shake.

Instead of returning my kind gesture, she raised her paw and said:

"Talk to the ~~hand~~ paw, girlfriend; the face don't want to hear it!"

"Say what?" I asked.

"I have a bone to pick with you, Indiana. I AM THE BABY IN THE FAMILY NOW, GOT IT?" Reese growled. And then she faded away.

"Indi! Indi! Indiana, wake up!" Harlow was yelling. "You are having a nightmare! Wake up!"

I opened my eyes. Oh, thank goodness! It was only a dream.

Later that day, I found Reese playing alone inside a cardboard box in the living room.

"Hi," I said, peeking my head into the box. "I'm Indiana."

Reese looked up at me with her big brown eyes and cute-as-a-button nose and said, "Hello, Banana. You are my big sister?"

Sigh. Children.

"No, Reese, my name is Indi–ana, not Banana. And yes, I guess I am your big sister."

"Good!" Reese said excitedly. "I was hoping you were. Pleased to meet you," she added, holding out her speckled little paw.

"Same," I mumbled.

And then Reese did the strangest thing. She gave me a kiss on the neck.

It startled me at first. I thought perhaps she might be a vampire going for my neck and that this was it for me. But I was wrong. Reese wasn't a vampire. Turns out she is the sweetest little polka–dotted creature I have ever met.

Just like that, I became a big sister. And Reese Lightning wasn't all that frightening.

TIPS FROM INDIANA

Take it from me, life with a new ~~baby~~ puppy is exhausting. If you are thinking of adding one to your family, here are a few things that you can expect:

① The new puppy will spend hours sleeping while you are wide awake. You might even wonder if your new puppy will ever wake up. (If you are really concerned, try poking your puppy with a small stick just to make sure it moves.)

The second that you are ready to call it a night, however, your new puppy will be just coming out of hibernation, ready to eat, play, and bite your ears. Good luck getting any rest with a new puppy in the house.

② Your new puppy will pick up on everything you do. If you pull a funny face in a family picture, the new puppy will copy~~cat~~dog you, which will result in no after-dinner treats for either one of you.

This can be a problem, but use it to your advantage and train your new puppy to pose for the camera. A photo is worth a thousand barks, and if you can snap a picture of your puppy looking cute, congratulations.

③ Your new puppy will not come trained or housebroken, and even if it is the middle of winter, you will have to teach it to go outside when it needs to do its business. FYI: puppies don't care for the cold, especially when their legs are short and their bellies touch the ground when they walk.

Get your puppy some cold-weather attire, teach it to be quick when it goes outside, and then, when you bring it in from the cold, bundle that puppy up and thaw out its little limbs! It will thank you after it defrosts.

SLEEPING LESSONS

Reese had a very strange sleeping schedule that
Harlow and I were having a hard time adjusting to.
In the daytime, Reese made herself comfortable
wherever she could (usually on Harlow's back) and
slept for hours on end.

Nighttime was a whole different story, and it was
because of the crate.

I thought I had seen the end of that little jail after I had boycotted it the year before. My parents had tried (unsuccessfully) to make me sleep in it before I was fully house-trained. As you can imagine, that didn't last long.

But for some reason, now they pulled it out of storage and were attempting to keep Reese in captivity while they slept at night. She wasn't having it any more than I did. And neither were Harlow and I.

While my parents slept peacefully, Harlow and I had to endure the crying and the howling.

"What, are they hard of hearing?" I asked Harlow in awe.

"Earplugs," Harlow replied. "This isn't their first rodeo. You were ten times worse."

"And what did you do?" I asked.

"Don't you remember, Indiana? I took matters into my own paws and I slept in the crate beside you. It was the only way to get you to sleep."

I had no recollection of this. But I took Harlow's story as a hint. For the sake of our sanity, I got into the crate with Reese and together we slept.

My little sister quit crying and cuddled right up to me. Problem solved.

The next morning, everyone was in a much happier mood.

And by the next week, we had shown Reese how to get what she wanted.

From that day forward, we all slept comfortably in our parents' bed.

OPPOSITES ATTRACT

It didn't take long for me to realize that Reese Lightning and I were very different. Polar opposites, actually.

Reese didn't try to steal my toys or my limelight. Getting attention seemed to be the last thing on her mind and she understood that everything was mine.

Unlike me, Reese doesn't ask a lot of questions. She doesn't worry about the what–ifs or the whys in life like I do.

"Where did your spots come from?" I asked her.

"I don't know. I was born this way," she replied.

"Reese, your body is all different colors, and to top it off, you have spots. Doesn't that bother you? Maybe if you have a bath or two, you will be able to make them disappear?"

"I like my spots. They make me unique!" she proclaimed. "Right, Harlow?"

"Right. That is a great attitude, Reese," Harlow said.

Reese and Harlow, on the other paw, were alike in every way.

Just like Harlow, Reese was non-confrontational. No matter what, I could not get that little animal to scuffle with me. I would steal her toys and her blankets. The only growl that I could get was from her stomach when I stole her treats.

It's not that I wanted to make her mad. I just wanted her to react. A little drama in the house never hurt anyone!

"What are you, Reese Lightning, America's sweetheart? Stop trying to be such a little saint!" I told her. But she couldn't help it. It was just in her nature.

Reese also knew the importance of telling the truth. Well, her big brown eyes did, anyway.

The little darling must have been feeling rebellious one day, because she surprised Harlow and me

by dragging a roll of toilet paper throughout the whole house. This was not her typical Goody Two-shoes behavior, but I wasn't going to stop her and neither was Harlow. Our little sister's first time toilet papering! We both watched her with proud smiles on our faces.

When my mother came home from running errands, Reese didn't try to blame Harlow and me for the mess like I would have done. Instead, she ratted herself out. It took one look at little Lightning for my mother to know that she was the culprit.

Even though we had our personality differences, Reese was getting more and more comfortable at my house and she seemed happy tagging along with Harlow and me, no matter what we did. When we wanted to catch some sunlight on the stairs, Reese was right there with us.

When we wanted to marathon-watch our favorite Meryl Streep movies, Reese took the front row.

It was as if the
three of us were
always meant to
be together.

THE ANIMALS UNDER THE FURNITURE

Reese was not very mischievous. I wanted to change that. She had such a small figure. I really felt like she should be taking advantage of what she could do with it, and so I decided to teach her a few tricks.

My father loves to eat treats. Not dog treats, but special treats made just for humans. So often I had watched as pieces of cookies, chips, and crackers fell between the cushions and onto the floor under his chair as he was eating. I wanted those treats so bad, and so did Harlow. The only problem was, we were too big to fit under the furniture. But Reese wasn't. She was still a bite-size puppy.

"You will sit here," I told Reese as I pointed with my nose to her position underneath the sofa. "Remember, don't eat anything. As soon as he is done, bring the treasures to us."

Harlow and I watched from across the room. My father was indulging in a bowl of popcorn and Reese had quite the pile of fallen goodies going on. *Such an obedient little angel!* I thought with pride.

When my father was done, he stood up and went upstairs.

I assumed Reese would come out, but she didn't.

And so we waited.

And waited.

"What is she doing under there?" Harlow asked.

I was starting to get worried. Did she get lost? I couldn't even see her anymore.

When it was time to go to bed, my father came back downstairs to round us up. "Bedtime, ladies!" he announced, looking at me and Harlow. "Where is your little sidekick?"

Harlow and I stared at the sofa.

"Reese?" he called. "Reese Lightning!"

"Keep staring, Indiana," Harlow told me. "Maybe he will get the hint."

Finally, my father lifted up the couch. And there she sat, with her big, full belly. She looked so happy.

"What are you doing?" my father asked as he picked Reese up.

I hurried to inspect. There were no treats left. Reese had eaten all of the popcorn pieces, plus a year's worth of crumbs. I was dumbfounded. "She didn't save us anything!" I told Harlow.

That was the night we realized that Reese Lightning could not be trusted to do our dirty work and that she REALLY loved to eat snacks.

"I am so full!" Reese whined as we got in bed to go to sleep.

"I can tell," I said, annoyed.

Reese's puppy clothes were beginning to burst at the seams.

Our family tradition on Christmas was to leave Santa Paws a plate of cookies and a glass of milk. I don't mean to ruin the fun, but . . . I am almost twelve in dog years. I stopped believing in Santa Paws a few months ago. Like, when I was nine.

Reese Lightning, however, still believed in Santa Paws, and so, being the best big sisters that we are, Harlow and I decided that it would be fun to surprise her on Christmas morning.

After Reese and my parents had fallen asleep on Christmas Eve, Harlow and I snuck downstairs to the living room. As usual, my mother had left the plate of cookies on the kitchen table, so we made sure to eat the whole thing before we went to the living room.

Our plan was to disguise Harlow as Santa Paws and have her hide behind the Christmas tree. When Reese would come downstairs to open presents the next morning—Surprise! Out would jump Harlow. Just like in an old classic Christmas movie!

Everything was going according to plan. We got Harlow into her costume and she looked amazing. I could hardly tell the difference between her and the fictional character that she was portraying. "Oh, Harlow! This is going to be perfect!" I told her.

"The best Christmas surprise ever!" she said excitedly.

When it was finally time to move Harlow to her position behind the tree, things got a little bit crazy.

"My paw! It's stuck!" she yelled.

Harlow had gotten her paw tangled up in the Christmas lights around the tree.

Untangling Harlow was a real struggle. (Dogs don't have opposable thumbs.) I was doing my best, but between the strands of lights and the decorations, I was only making things worse.

And that is when it happened.

Our tree came crashing down to the ground, right on top of the both of us.

My father came running down to the living room, followed by my upset mother and a confused little Reese.

"What is going on?" my father demanded as he lifted the tree off of us. "What are you two doing?"

I hid behind Harlow. "She did it!" I yelled.

"Don't you bark at me, Indiana!" my father yelled back. "And Harlow, what are you wearing? Why are you dressed like that? How did you get that on?"

(So embarrassing.)

Meanwhile, in the midst of the chaos, nobody noticed that Reese was tearing through all the wrapped presents.

"I love Christmas!" she said as she unwrapped each one.

Harlow and I spent Christmas Day in time-out while Reese got to enjoy her new toys beside the tipped-over tree. And just like in a classic Christmas movie, it was the perfect Christmas disaster.

NEW YEAR'S

Harlow, Reese, and I spent New Year's Eve doing
what everyone else does.

Sleeping.

And we spent New Year's Day doing what
everyone else does.

Celebrating.

LIFE LESSONS

Just like Harlow had done for me when I was a small pup, and just as Sage had done for Harlow when she was a small pup, I decided to take little Reese Lightning under my wing and teach her some of life's most valuable lessons.

When Harlow trained me, she had started with **sharing**, so that was right where I began.

The month of January in our house is dedicated to this one silly little occasion that takes place every year: Harlow's birthday.

I love Harlow, but come on! Does she really need a whole month?

Humble old Harlow plays it cool every other month of the year, but during January, she turns into a total diva. This year, when the big day rolled around, I thought it would be a great way to teach Reese how to share.

Harlow was still sound asleep. *Beauty rest,* I thought. (And she needs it too! Another year meant another gray hair in her coat, and she has so many already.)

102

"Okay, Reese, today is Harlow's special day. Usually on someone's birthday, they get presents, cake, balloons, and everyone's attention. But today it's going to be all about you!" I quietly explained.

"It is?" Reese asked.

"Yes, Reese, it is!"

"But won't Harlow be sad?" Reese asked.

I hadn't thought of that. "Reese, sometimes in life you have to learn to share. Harlow will probably be happy to share her special day with you," I explained. "Do you understand?"

"I guess so," she replied.

We snuck down to the kitchen while everyone slept peacefully upstairs. It was early and I wasn't usually a morning person, but a day like today called for it.

Harlow's presents were beautifully displayed all over the kitchen. Right next to them sat a cake. Gluten-free, of course. (Harlow thinks she has a gluten intolerance.)

After seeing how much Reese enjoyed opening presents on Christmas morning, I knew she would be a pro at unwrapping all of Harlow's birthday gifts.

"What are you waiting for? Dig in, Reese!" I told her.

Once again, she hesitated. "I don't know, Indi," she said. "I think Harlow will be mad when she wakes up."

Ugh, little Reese Lightning. So thoughtful. So pure of heart.

"Reese, I am your big sister. Would I ever tell you that it was okay to do something if it wasn't?" I asked. "Would a big sister ever ask you to do something that would get you in trouble? No! Besides, Harlow told me it would be fine."

"She did?" Reese asked.

"Yes! Now, go crazy!" I told her.

And that is just what she did. (I helped.)

After every present had been unwrapped and we had eaten enough cake to never want to eat cake again, we fell into a party coma on the couch.

A few hours later, we woke up to the sound of barking.

Uh-oh, I thought.

When Reese and I walked into the kitchen to see what Harlow was barking about, it took one look from Harlow for me to realize that I was in the doghouse.

"You ruined my day," Harlow said sadly.

(If that's not enough to break your heart,
I don't know what is!)

"But Harlow! I was trying to teach Reese how to
share! It was a lesson," I told her.

"Reese was in on this too?"
she asked, staring at Reese.

I wanted to lie. For the first time in my life,
I wanted to take all of the blame. But when I looked
over at Reese, I knew that I couldn't. Not because
I didn't want to, but because Reese's face was
covered with cake frosting.

"I WAS TEACHING HER A LESSON!"
I said again. Louder this time, in case she hadn't heard the first time.

"Indiana," Harlow yelled. "That is not the way things work. Stealing someone's special day is not sharing. It's stealing! You takin' notes, little one?" Harlow said, looking down at Reese.

Reese nodded. She was hiding behind me.

"Good!" Harlow said. "You will get your next lesson in sharing on Indiana's special day."

"Wait . . . What?" I asked.

Harlow didn't reply. Instead, she sat down and finished what was left of her gluten-free cake.

MONDAYS

I don't know if anyone else can relate, but . . . Mondays are a very difficult day at my house.

My parents are so noisy when they wake up early to go to work. After two days of uninterrupted rest, it can be so frustrating for those of us who are just lying around, trying to get some shut-eye!

"Quiet!" I yell at my mother as she turns on her noisy hair gun and dries her mane. On any other day of the week, I might try to fight with the hair gun, but not on a Monday. Nothing productive ever takes place on Mondays.

Reese Lightning learned quickly that Harlow and I did not play around on Mondays. She tried to share her obnoxious puppy energy with us, but Harlow and I weren't having it.

"Stop it," Harlow would warn, as Reese bit at her face.

"Waaaaake up!" Reese would whine.

At first she found ways to entertain herself: trying to eat her own toes and playing alone with her babies in the hallway. But eventually she saw how unnecessary Mondays are and started to dislike them just as much as the rest of us did.

The best way to handle a Monday is to curl up in bed and sleep until Tuesday.

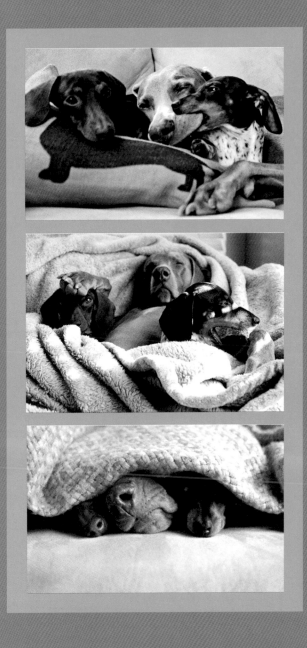

THE BATH

Call me crazy, but I think that bath time is a weekly ritual that we could all do without. (The fact that humans practice this daily is enough to give me an ulcer!)

If Reese and I have only one thing in common it is that we both despise getting our fur wet.

Harlow is the opposite. She loves the bath. Do you want to know why? She has webbed feet! (Please don't tell her that I told you. She would be so embarrassed if she knew that I was talking about her feet.)

I have never heard sweet little Reese raise her voice. I honestly didn't think she had it in her . . . until the day my parents put her in the bathtub.

"Hellllp meeeeee!" she screamed, paddling her stubby little legs in the air. She wasn't even touching the water yet, and already she knew the terror that was coming.

"You are okay, Reese!" my parents told her.

"Take a deep breath, little one," Harlow encouraged.

While all of this nonsense was taking place in the washroom, I hid quietly under the bed. I knew what was coming. Just like in the plot of a scary movie, I was next.

The moment Reese's feet were back on solid ground, she took off running.

"AHHHHHHH!" she screamed as she ran from room to room.

What an entertaining little performance, I thought. She was taking this harder than I ever had.

My parents probably thought Reese would adapt to the bath and that over time she would be a better sport about it, but boy were they wrong. As time went by, Reese got worse. Just the sound of running water was enough to throw her into shock.

I can't remember whose brilliant idea it was, but one of my parents suggested putting me in the bath with her. Yes, it helped calm Reese down, but . . . um, no, thank you. Can you imagine taking a bath with your siblings? How mortifying!

PUPPY'S DAY OUT

"I had the strangest dream last night," Reese said one morning over kibble and coffee. "I dreamt that I snuck onto an airplane and ended up in New York City! The next thing I knew, I was all alone, lost in Central Park."

Reese had taken a sudden interest in traveling. For a pup that was usually so cautious and shy, she had become obsessed with seeking adventure.

"Were you scared?" I asked. "In your dream?"

"No. I was feeding the birds, exploring the territory. It was a real good time!" she said excitedly.

"Reese, Central Park is very far away. It is also a big place for such a small little animal like you. Why don't you think of other places that you can visit? Places close to home," I told her.

"Like where?" she asked.

"Well, why don't you and I go out on a little adventure today?" I asked.

My parents were both working and Harlow was still in bed. "Killer migraine," she'd said when I had tried to wake her up for breakfast.

It was the perfect day for Reese and I to go out for some sisterly bonding.

"Really, Indi?" Reese screamed. "A real adventure? But how will we get around? We can't drive."

"Oh, Reese, don't be silly. We don't need a car to go on an adventure!" I told her.

Our first stop: the pet store. I wanted to show Reese the amphibians. She had never seen them in real life before. (Also, we were out of dog food.)

Everyone at our neighborhood pet shop thought that Reese and I were adorable.

"Well, hello, little angels!" the cashier said when we paid for our items.

"Watch it, lady!" I warned. "We aren't little!"

"Strangers are so strange," Reese whispered to me.

"Now what would you like to do?" I asked Reese when we got outside.

Reese's eyes lit up when she saw the ice-cream truck parked across the street.

"I have always wanted to try ice cream," Reese said quietly. "Oh, please, Indi?"

She really knew how to work those big puppy eyes when she needed to. Who on earth could ever say no to her?

I have never had to ask a stranger for food, so I was really stepping outside of my comfort zone when I wandered up to the ice-cream truck. Millions of children were swarming it, so I got in line. I wasn't sure what to do, so I decided to just try to blend in. I stood on two legs and tried to speak.

Now, I am not sure if the ice-cream man was some sort of genius and understood me or if he could just read minds, but he gave me exactly what I wanted.

"Thank you, Indi!" Reese squealed in excitement when I handed her the cone.

"Anytime, babe!" I replied.

I really had this big–sister
business down!

We finished our adventure with a trip to the dog park. (I was just dying to use the facilities!)

"This right here is a slide, Reese," I explained. "Children know how to go down them while sitting, because most children don't have to worry about smashing their tails."

"Children don't have tails?" Reese asked, concerned.

"I have never seen a child with a tail," I replied.

"Children are so strange," Reese said under her breath.

On our way home from the park, we ran into the neighbor girls, Pig and Cindy. Reese was fixated on Cindy's hair.

"Stop staring, Reese. It's rude," I whispered to her as we walked by them.

"But it has a ponytail on top of its head!" she exclaimed.

(FYI: There is something about dogs styling their own hair that really frightens other dogs.)

When we finally got home, Harlow was sitting on the front porch. She didn't look as happy to see us as I had hoped she would.

"What were you thinking? Going out without your leashes and a responsible adult? You know the rules, Indi! That's naughty! I hope you two had fun!" Harlow yelled as she turned around and went back inside the house.

"Harlow is so strange," Reese said and laughed.

"Remind me to never act like that when I get old," I told Reese.

"Today was the best day of my life!" Reese announced.

"Mine too," I replied.

Later that night, after Harlow had settled down, I apologized and gave her some of the treats that we had picked up during our outing.

Moral of the story:
If you are going to
sneak out, make sure
to take your leash and
always return home
with something sweet
for your babysitter,
parent(s), or legal
guardian(s).

When springtime rolled around and the snow had melted off the ground, I knew that it was time for our family's annual camping trip.

I think I might have been a grizzly bear in my former life, because there is nothing I love more than the great outdoors! Fresh mountain air, birds chirping, the smell of marshmallows roasting on a campfire. Can you imagine anything better? I was born to camp!

"Indiana, why are you so excited? You have never spent more than forty-five minutes in the great outdoors," Harlow said.

Unfortunately, this was true. Our First Annual Camping Trip was cut short because I had an accident in the tent. (I was only six months old! Give me a break!)

We found the perfect camping spot between two beautiful pines.

"This is it, darlings!" I told my two sisters as we got out of the car. "This is where a weekend of fun-filled adventure and a lifetime of memories begins."

"Yeah, yeah, Indiana. We will see," Harlow said.

Reese Lightning was one happy camper. During our family walk, she had her nose in everything.

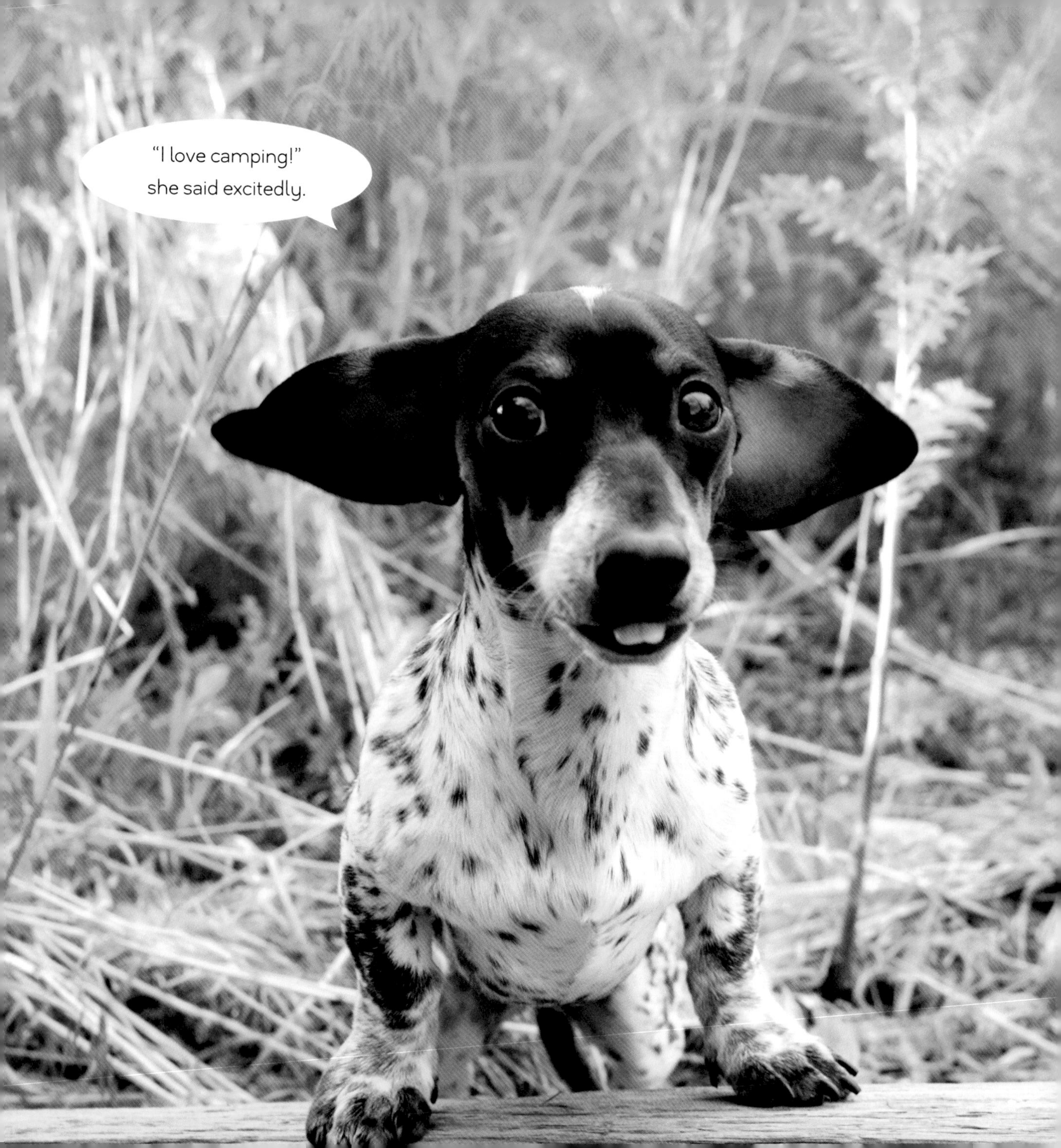
"I love camping!" she said excitedly.

"Listen to her barking!" my father whispered to my mother. "I think she likes it here!"

Reese never got in trouble for barking. "She's just trying to find her voice," my mother had once explained. I always wondered where she'd lost it . . .

While my parents prepared our dinner, Harlow, Reese, and I decided to do some exploring on our own.

"Don't go too far, ladies," my father yelled. "Stay close to Harlow."

Harlow looked down and said to me and Reese, "No funny business, you two."

That Harlow—she could be such a fun-sponge sometimes!

"What is your favorite part about camping so far, Reese?" I asked as we walked.

"The sticks," she said without thinking.

Just like Harlow, Reese loves sticks. (Weirdos.)

When we found a lake, Harlow just couldn't help herself. She dove right in!

"Oh, my, cold!" she screamed as she ran out.

"You are crazy!" I said, shaking my head.

"I dare you to get your paws wet, Indiana," Reese said.

"Oh, I don't know. I am not really in the mood," I said. No way was I getting into lake water. I saw a documentary once about some sort of monster that lived in a lake. It survived by eating small creatures and seaweed. I was not going to take my chances.

"I think our hotdogs are done cooking. Let's head back," Harlow said.

"Don't you think it's funny that we are having hot*dogs* for dinner?" I asked.

"No. Why would it be?" Harlow asked, confused.

"I love hotdogs!" Reese chimed in.

(Being the smartest dog in the family was so worrying sometimes.)

On our way back to the campsite, we ran into trouble.

"Oh, no," Harlow said when she saw it.

On the trail directly in front of us was a skunk.

Harlow and I both turned to Reese, but it was too late. She was running for it.

"No, Reese! Stop!" I yelled as Harlow tried to chase after her.

Ever since she was little, Reese's favorite baby had been her stuffed skunk, Roxanne.

"Roxanne!" Reese screamed as she ran toward the real skunk.

Either this skunk didn't like being referred to as Roxanne or it was scared that my sweet little sister was a rabid beast. Whatever the case, it lifted its tail and sprayed Reese Lightning in the face.

The smell of Reese was awful and enough to keep my parents from wanting to share a small tent with her for the next two days, so they packed everything up and we went home.

Our Second Annual Camping Trip had lasted exactly twelve minutes longer than our First Annual Camping Trip.

THREE'S COMPANY

As puppies do, mine was growing up.

During her routine vet checkup last week, Reese Lightning topped the scales at a whopping four pounds! (Can that little lady get a round of appaws?)

"Oh, Harlow!" I said with sadness. "Soon our little darling will be ready to leave the nest!"

"No, she won't!" Harlow laughed. "Dogs don't work like that, Indiana. She is here with us for good!"

"Wait. What?" I said, trying to sound surprised. "I thought for sure she would be ready to find her own home by the time she was six months old? Isn't that when humans leave the nest? At six months old?"

Harlow and I both started to laugh.

It is true that in the beginning I had my doubts about Reese Lightning. Those first few weeks really were frightening! But now I don't think I could live without the Little Bo Peep!

Reese has always looked up to Harlow and me. I mean, literally, she has always had to look up to see us. (Short-dog problems!) These days, however, Harlow and I were starting to learn a thing or two from our baby sister.

"Indiana, who is your best friend?" Reese asked one day when we were sitting around, having a cuddle. I was sandwiched right between the two of them. "Me or Harlow?"

I didn't reply. If I said that Reese was my best friend, I would hurt Harlow's feelings. And if I said that Harlow was my best friend, I would hurt Reese's feelings.

To be fair, though, I honestly couldn't choose between the two.

"It's okay, Indiana. You don't have to choose," Reese said. "I know that you like us both the same. We are both special to you in our own different ways."

Such a small brain Reese had, yet full of so much wisdom!

"Why did you ask if you already knew the answer, Reese?" Harlow asked.

"So that I could see Indiana get nervous and blush!" Reese said excitedly.

"You can't see me blushing!" I said, embarrassed. "I have fur on my face!"

"Actually, Indiana, I can tell when you are," Harlow said.

"Yeah, me too!" Reese agreed.

"Quit mocking me!" I yelled.

"Indiana! Quit your barking!" my mother yelled from the next room.

"Oh, Indiana! We are only trying to get under your fur," Harlow said jokingly, and the three of us howled with laughter.

HARLOW, INDIANA, AND REESE

During the first year of my life, it was just me and my Harlow. I thought everything was perfect. And it was; I had the best friend on planet Earth.

But then life got even more perfect when Reese came along.

She was the greatest addition to our pack and the best little sister that Harlow and I could ever ask for.

Who would have thought that becoming a middle child would be so lovely? My parents love me the same, everyone still thinks that I am the ~~cat's~~ dog's meow, and now I have not one but two best friends—a big sister to keep me out of trouble and a little sister with whom I can cause trouble! I am very lucky.

And that is it. The middle of our story. The beginning of Reese's story.

We will be back when we have more
adventures to share.

Good-bye.

ACKNOWLEDGMENTS

Harlow, Indiana, and Reese bring so much joy to our lives and we feel blessed for the opportunity to tell their story. Every day with them is an adventure that we feel grateful to be on.

Thank you, Harlow, Indiana, and Reese, for letting us be your roommates/parents. Thank you for making us laugh and cry (when you chew up our belongings!). And thank you for making our hearts feel so full.

Sharing our dogs and their story would not be possible without the following three people:

Dan Toffey

Rachel Vogel

Kerri Kolen

We will never be able to thank each one of you enough. You three are the best.

Sofie Brooks, Katie McKee, and everyone at Putnam and Waxman Leavell, thank you for all of your kindness and for all of the time that you have spent making this book come to life.

To our family and friends: Thank you for loving our dogs just as much as we do and for taking such good care of them when they are in your paws. Harlow, Indiana, and Reese have the world's best grandparents, who we don't know what we would do without.

Last but certainly not least, thank you to all of Harlow, Indiana, and Reese's followers, fans, and friends. We are so thankful for all of your love and support. We hope you are having as much fun as we are.